TO THE EXTREME

Skateboarding

by Matt Doeden

Reading Consultant:
Barbara J. Fox
Reading Specialist
North Carolina State University

Capstone
press

Mankato, Minnesota

Blazers is published by Capstone Press
151 Good Counsel Drive, P.O. Box 669, Mankato, Minnesota 56002
www.capstonepress.com

Library of Congress Cataloging-in-Publication Data
Doeden, Matt.
    Skateboarding / by Matt Doeden.
    p. cm.—(Blazers. To the extreme)
    Includes bibliographical references and index.
    ISBN 0-7368-2730-7 (hardcover)
    1. Skateboarding—Juvenile literature. [1. Skateboarding.
2. Extreme sports.] I. Title II. Series: Doeden, Matt. Blazers.
To the extreme.
GV859.8.D63 2005
796.22—dc22   2003026627

Summary: Describes the sport of skateboarding, including tricks and
    safety information.

Editorial Credits
Angela Kaelberer, editor; Jason Knudson, designer; Jo Miller,
    photo researcher; Eric Kudalis, product planning editor

Photo Credits
Capstone Press/Gary Sundermeyer, 26
Corbis/Duomo, 7, 8, 28–29; NewSport/Al Fuchs, 5, 12; NewSport/
    Rick Rickman, 25; NewSport/X Games IX/Matt A.Brown, 19
Getty Images/Elsa, 11, 20 (left), 22; Ezra Shaw, cover, 23;
    Stanley Chou, 13, 21 (right)
Index Stock Imagery/Barry Winiker, 16–17
Mira/Carl Schneider, 20–21; Mira/Todd Powell Photography, 15

1 2 3 4 5 6 09 08 07 06 05 04

Table of Contents

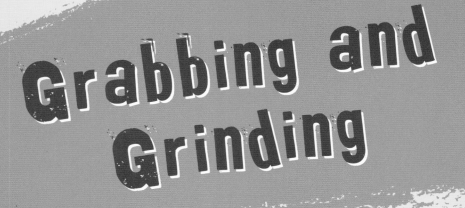

Grabbing and Grinding

A skater speeds down a halfpipe ramp. He glides up the other side. The skater reaches the top of the ramp. He sails high into the air.

4

The skater is high above the ramp. He reaches for his board to spin it in the air. This trick is called a varial.

A halfpipe ramp is U-shaped.

Halfpipe ramp

The skater lands on his board. He speeds down the ramp. He is ready to do another trick.

BLAZER FACT

In 2002, skater Danny Way set a world record by jumping 18 feet, 3 inches (5.5 meters) above a ramp.

Skateboards

The deck is the main part of the skateboard. Most skateboard decks are made of wood.

Metal parts called trucks are
under the deck. The trucks connect
the wheels to the deck.

Truck

Wheel

Skateboard wheels are made of urethane. The wheels grip ramps, concrete bowls, and pavement.

BLAZER FACT

Years ago, skaters practiced in empty swimming pools.

Concrete bowl

Skatepark Diagram

Coping

Quarterpipe ramps

Fun box

Jump ramp

Slide rail

17

Tricks

Most skateboarding tricks begin with an ollie. Skaters step hard on the board's tail. The board then pops into the air.

Tail

Kickflip

Many skaters do street tricks.
Skaters do kickflips off benches.
They slide and grind along rails.

Slide

Grind

Coping

Skaters perform vert tricks off
large halfpipe ramps. Skaters do
spins, flips, and grabs. They grind on
the coping.

Grab

safety

Falls are part of skateboarding. Helmets, elbow pads, and knee pads help protect skaters.

Some skaters build their own ramps. Others do grabs and grinds at skateparks. Safe skating places help skaters stay on the ramps, instead of on the sidelines.

BLAZER FACT

Each year, skateboarding injuries send about 50,000 skaters to U.S. hospital emergency rooms.

Grinding the coping